MW01101475

#themikeboard

By Mike Maeshiro

ISBN:978-0-9987358-0-1

DEDICATION

This book is dedicated to my dear mother,
Kim Maeshiro. She taught me the value of
poetry, the written word and the English
language. Thank you for the loving care with
which you raised me and the spirit of
celebration you host so well.
I love you.

ACKNOWLEDGMENTS

I'd like to thank the Holy Spirit for being such a kind
and faithful friend, Emily Ables for your watchful eye
and artistic excellence in making this book look fantastic,
Janna Gilbertson for your consistency and dedication
throughout the whole process, and the rest of
my team. We changed the world together,
thank you for saying yes.

INTRODUCTION

Truth is a Person;
He doesn't become something He's not,
nor does He cease being what He is. He is not
dictated by facts or words, quite the contrary is
true. In this book, you will read definitive statements
in the declarative form. Some of them will challenge
what you already believe...if you let them. I would
encourage you, as you read the excerpts in this book,
to not judge them based on whether you agree
immediately or not. Judge the writings here on
whether they can open you up to the Person of Truth.
Engaging with Truth is not a passive experience,
we must contend to understand Him.
These writings aim to provide the wrestling arena,
you must step into the ring. The agreements
you've made in the spiritual realm, in your
subconscious and in your emotions will be
provoked...if you let them.
Don't just agree or disagree, grow.
Let this book open you up to new possibilities
or close doors that don't serve you.
Happy hunting!

CONTENTS

LOVE

The trusting nature of love disarms the heart
and awakens, within another, what it holds most
dear in itself.

Standards are structures to uphold excellence,
not reasons to withhold love.

Gentleness seems weak and vulnerable to
the insecure but is the only way love chooses to
touch the world. Love is the most
secure place in existence.

No one is big enough for you.
There is not a person beautiful enough, smart
enough, strong enough, kind enough or rich
enough. Even if you believe they are, your
appetite will betray you; they will fail. You were
made to house the divine. The ache you feel in
your soul, that emptiness, that ravenous hunger,
it can only be satisfied by something beyond
you, something greater, something higher.
To feed off of another mortal is cannibalistic.
The chasm of your need for love cannot be
filled by anything shorter than God Himself.
Yes, you're that deep. It is His heart that must
touch yours, it is His breath with which you
must inhale; His words, His kisses.
And when it's Him you pull from, even the
lowest being is enough. The ugliest person is
beautiful enough, the dumbest person
is smart enough, the weakest person
is strong enough, the meanest person is kind
enough, the poorest person is rich enough.

The
security
of
LOVE
is
not
needing
any.

If you don't know love, what you
DO know is worthless.

If you get quiet enough and you wait long enough,
you will notice hope lighting upon your soul
and love Himself lilting inside of you.
You are loved at all times, in every moment.
Do yourself a favor and enjoy Him.
What a gracious, kind and faithful friend.

It moved me to tears when He said He loved me
because somehow I was privileged to
know He meant it.

An honest heart doesn't need offense because
it has the power of truth to protect it,
this is where humility is born.

Love frightens us with the thrill of being intimately
known while removing the fear of anything else.

There is no demand in love, just passionate celebration.

There isn't a dropper of love from which you pull,
you are in an ocean; the stopper you believe
in is from within.

the
world.

You don't fight your way to love, you surrender.

Do you need help recognizing when love knocks?
He feels like giving. Giving up, giving in, giving away
who you are. Love spends, love spills. That
temptation to retract and withhold, love is
probably doing the opposite.

Love makes no demand but offers Himself.

Love attracts solutions and builds answers.

Love doesn't look to see what is beautiful, love brings beauty and finds recipients upon whom to cast its light.

If love is too expensive, we are broke
in the truest measure.

Don't be afraid of love, He's the riskiest safeguard
and the most trustworthy gamble.

There's

somebody

inside of

me

called Love

who needs

to

touch

people

and He uses my body

to do

it.

Get right up in the way of love. You don't need to
chase love down, He's too big to catch. He moves.
But if you get in His way, He will sweep you up into
the blustery wind of His movement and it is delicious.

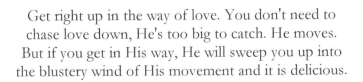

You are a lover who works, not the other way around.

What good is your help if your heart is far away?
What good is your wisdom if your love is absent?
What good is your strength if your affection is missing?
Do not speak if love does not compel you, do not
help if you do not care.

Fear is selfish.
Only love can convince you the risk is worth it.

You don't have to offer yourself to God.
Enjoy Him, explore Him. As you delight in Him,
He will eat you up. You won't need to crawl onto
any altar, He's not looking for a sacrifice.
You're his lover, you don't have to
convince Him you're desirable.
He wants you. Enjoy him for yourself,
He knows how to enjoy you.

FUN

Fun is the door to the authentic you.

Wealth is not a matter of resources but appreciation.
We are all filthy rich.

Blessed are they who play, for they know things about
the game the others will never.

This is a game of winning, not watching.
And you will win. It's in the cards. You weren't
dealt a winning or losing hand, you were seated
at a different table. At this table, it doesn't
matter your hand, the game is set for you to win.
You don't play for chips or money, you play
for fun, for the thrill of the game, because the
owner of the house is hidden in the play.
The glory of God cannot just be observed,
it must be felt, experienced; it
must be transcendent.

It's
only
tiring
if
you
don't
care
about
it.

Our innocence is expressed most honestly through joy.
The original you is happy.

You were built to burn. You're allergic to stale
and rigid. It is in the fire that your glory comes forth.
Dance into the dizzying vulnerability and revelry of
doing things because they're fun, because you enjoy
them. Serve the world with your passion, meet
needs with your creativity and money will be
thrown at your feet, influence will bow to you
and your head will raise to meet the sunlight
with full reception. You were built for the light.
Follow love into the brightness.

There is power, like creative energy, that is
Knocking on your soul to be harnessed.
The power in the world wants to be used.
It is a willing, zealous servant and it wants to
fulfill its destiny. Honor it: create.

Creativity and imagination can take our deepest longings to places our judgments would never permit them. In this vulnerability is the door to our dreams.

Don't just give what you have, give it with fervor and gusto! If you fall, let it end in an explosion. If you soar, let it be a blazing trajectory! Do not waddle, erupt.

I've noticed my ability to genuinely celebrate other people's victories dramatically increased when I started having victories of my own. It's important that you win in your own life so you can fully show up in the lives of those around you.

Our

dreams

are

our

liberation

from

the

lies

we've

been

told.

You're a child, true maturity doesn't hide this but embraces it. Let the child play!

Joy is not something you fight for, it's a place you live from. Those of you who turn joy into a task, stop it. You don't practice joy, you host Him.

Don't forget to have fun. If you're not having fun, something will break. You can be the one to choose what breaks.

Don't be concerned with them liking what you create, YOU like it; show them the way.

Joy isn't just for the simple, it's for the brokenhearted, the confused, the angry, and for anyone who is a person. We laugh because God laughs. Celebrate the laughter of others and join in if you're able.

Your calling is to enjoy who you are and what you have. We're able to do this because of Who we're found in. We are hidden in Mr. Joy. If you're not having fun, you're being robbed. Get it together.

boredom

is the result of falsehood.

God is playing hide and seek with us and He has given us some tools to find Him. One is wonder, one is awe, another is called "with all your heart."

A cubicle can only be a temporary solution, not a lifestyle choice. There is nothing natural about a fabric-laden box within which a human being is meant to reside happily.
Expand.

His plan for you is electric with life and adventure and hope and love and fun. Catch a glimpse and blaze that trail.

"Have to," "need to," "should..." Boo.
Life is a passion to drink, not a law to be
written. Forget compulsion or obligation.
Stand up and live your life. You owe nothing
to no one but love. This is a fiery ordeal,
not a wet blanket to abide.

We are always anticipating what is to come
in the future but we must learn how to enjoy the
present. The future will always be there and will
always be unattainable; it's fun to look at but
will never be ours. The present is here, available
and ready. Don't rush, don't spend, don't fight,
revel. The beauty of the world is in this moment,
He's here and He's to be delighted in.

The most responsible thing you can do as
a person is enjoy.

Let the expression of jubilance and celebration
come out of you, give it form and voice. If you hold
it in, if you hide it, it will die. When we fail to express
joy, we withhold the seed that impregnates the air
with acceptance and approval.

The healthiest you is having fun, there is no
such thing as joyless vitality.

SIGNIFICANCE

It doesn't matter whether or not you are enough.
Once you realize that, you become more than anyone
could ask for.

You are brilliant. You do not fail because of
inadequacy or lack, you fail because of ignorance.

There is so much potential all around you.
To see it, you must first see it in yourself. The world
is a reflection, after all.

Comparison only comes when we lose faith in who we are. Don't try to beat anyone out, beat out the lameness of your own beliefs. You. Are. Awesome.

One of the greater deceptions is that we are alone in our pain. We falsely take ownership over hurt that doesn't just belong to us. We are part of a greater whole. Your pain belongs to our people. #community

What you believe about yourself determines what you will permit to come into your life. There are things we think we want that exceed our belief in ourselves. When the time comes to appropriate them, we will sabotage the possibility. Dreaming is sourced from within. Love yourself! It is you who will steward the manifestation of your desire.

You can't consider someone as better than yourself
if you don't know your own worth.

A victim is aware of what they can't do and what
they don't want...of who they aren't. A hero is
driven by who they are, pulled by what they do want,
and so, discover what they can do. The gospel
pronounces the end of the victim; our victim was
crucified with Christ. Our desire is designed
to pull us. When we follow our God-given
desire, we encounter many things we don't want.
A hero doesn't keep track of what they don't want.
They learn how to overcome. It is unnatural
for us to set up camp around what we hate or
to focus on what we can't do; it is unnatural
for us to be persuaded of who we aren't

You are eligible for friendship with God. Any
smallness you feel contradicts your nature. Your
potential is communion with the infinite.

I didn't know it was going to be this good. I didn't know getting to be me was going to be so rewarding. I didn't know my dreams weren't as far away as they felt. I didn't realize the difficulties would make life easier, I didn't realize the overcoming would cause me to become more. I didn't realize I would be able to trust people like this, I didn't realize I would be loved like this, I didn't realize I could be celebrated this well. Things can be hard, but people can be so wrong about how hard they are. I was told the world was bad, people are dangerous, I'm inherently wicked and I would have to struggle most of my life. I didn't realize I was hearing lies for so long. I was told I was special, I didn't realize how special. I was told I was going to change the world, I didn't realize how malleable the world is. I didn't realize love was so close and abundant, I didn't know life could be this good.

Never

accept

the

counsel

of someone

who gives

you

permission

to be less

than who

you

really

are.

In a world of noise and busy-ness, you must be a person of clarity and focus. Whatever your message, commit to it. Whatever your voice, sing.

The idea that you're not there, that you haven't arrived is anti-gospel. The reality is you were never going to arrive, that was never going to happen. Stop looking for the ways you don't measure up so you can try to fill the gap, you can't fill it! Stop looking for the reasons you're not enough, you can't be enough.

The light of a brilliant star doesn't diminish the light of your own, it only validates that shining is what you do and you are among those who shine.

Your job is to explore, discover, recognize and embrace who God is in you and then do not deny Him.

You're so valuable. When you're convinced of this, the world will ask you to come out and play. When you catch the light inside of you, the world clears space and sets you a stage. The world wants what you bring to the table, only believe.

It doesn't need to be perfect timing, it doesn't need to be perfectly said, it doesn't need to be perfectly executed, it just needs to be perfectly yours.

What life has broken, let life restore. You are not a piece, you are alive. Though shape and form may vary, know this: God is in you, vessel. Snapped, disjointed, misplaced, incomplete. These words are far from you, only knowing defeat. You are alive, therefore beautiful. You grow, therefore become. You're perfect. Though your journey has seasons and patterns, your substance is renewed, your makeup divine. Do not despise the formation of the story for in it your beauty is revealed, and the pinnacle of that beauty is that it was never yours to begin with. To revel in the glory revealed in you as belonging to Him is the ultimate exultation, He and you are one. You're perfect.

Remember who you are and what you have to
give. In this changing world with endless opportunities,
relationships and experiences, give your heart away.
You have something to offer and it's more
blessed to do so.

I don't go out to work anymore, I go out to build.
I don't look for a job, I look for impact. I'm not looking
for someone to hire me, I'm looking to influence.

Success is a mastery of who you are; an ownership
that leads to celebration. When this is your experience,
you are successful. The world throws money
at these people.

If you need a microphone to have something profound to say, you will never have something profound to say nor will you have the mic. If you can see past the microphone and shine without the spotlight, you'll discover your own profundity and the lights will highlight you. But the biggest reward is that what you have will be yours. You'll enjoy it without their permission and when you give it away, they won't be able to stop it.

You have been made with infinite value,
you are worth God's life. He's smitten and the
dirty or inadequate that you see or feel in your
life is simply irrelevant to who you are.
Precious you, you're caught
in heaven's kiss; in the heart
of the Highest One.

God shows you
who you are
so you can show them

who **He** is.

We must refuse to settle for anything less than tireless originality. It's appropriate to copy others for means of efficiency or accuracy but never to express ourselves. Who we are and what we feel is so contingent upon our unique design, it is to sacrifice the preciousness of identity to borrow someone else's choice.

Serving was never designed to be indifferent or impersonal, we cannot serve apart from who we are. Our talent uniquely sets us up to serve with a certain fierceness and efficiency. This power is regulated by the degree to which we embrace what we have been given. Do not downplay your gift. You will influence the most people the most completely by adhering to your unique design. Give who you are in your purest flavor. It's by your talent you have been equipped to change the world.

Sometimes we find ourselves waiting for a rescuer, someone who will come and save us from our own lives. The truth is, that person doesn't exist. There is no knight in shining armor because there is no damsel in distress, there are no victims in this kingdom. You see, the rescue already happened, the knight already came. He slayed the dragon and rescued the fair maiden from the pit. She goes by a different name now and she has been given a new role. She is no longer a lady in waiting, she has been given a sword and a map. She has been empowered to advance and take ground in the land of the heart. You are her. The rescue mission is over. Stop waiting for a hero and stand up. You ARE the hero. No one is coming. There are companions along the way but your victory will be wrought by your hand. The King has seen to it. In His kingdom, no one is powerless and no one lacks. To trust Him is to believe in the power He gave you. It's called identity and choice. Now go, choose. Be. Stand.

You are not in the way...
you *are* His way.

Your personality is God's pathway
to your heart.

Don't hope for change, hope for the power to be fully you. When you show up with all that you are, the power you carry forces circumstances to change. Wake up and realize it's not what you do but what you are convinced of that moves mountains.

You are not small, do not be fooled. You occupy more than your eyes can see. There is nothing small about love, for it is the source and fabric of life and He has taken up residence in your being. You are not separate, the Divine is in your heart. You're huge.

The world will never discover the beauty you have to offer if you don't. Your gift is not just for you, expose it to the light and it will feed the people.

Don't give up on your dreams. Even if it's inconvenient, make a path for your dreams to breathe. Without you, they will never be born.

Our dreams are not our responsibility but a gift to us. In what we want, divinity touches our humanity and kisses us in the language of experience. May we have the guts to stand in that arena and hold our ground, refusing to budge from our heart's desire. We will not rest until what we want is what we have.

Resist the temptation to hide behind someone else's power in your life. You are empowered as an individual, what you carry is beautiful and specific. You must embrace it, own it, in order to authentically give it away. Your ability to love is contingent upon your ability to take responsibility for yourself.

If you put effort and intention into choosing better, in whatever area, it is important that you catch the little moments that speak of progress. They come and go so quietly, so subtly, so unannounced. Being the steward of your choices, it is your responsibility to catch those victories and give them the appropriate level of attention and celebration.

Tall is the man and brave is he who sees himself as he is and is that man before every man.

Be bigger than life. You're large on the inside, so just be honest and wow the world! Every single one of us is weird. The only "normal" ones are lying and they've forfeited their power to change the world. Go big, it's the truth.

FEAR

There's nothing like the threat of religion to choke the joy out of life and punish the wrongdoer for his deviant ways. You know what God did with the wrongdoer when He lived here? He loved them. He forgave them. He partied with them. Do you think a flower is concerned with its adherence to the rules of being a flower? Do you think the robin is ashamed of its song? Do you think the sunset is afraid of being punished? God killed punishment, you're genuinely free. Let go of the restrictions fear has taught you to leverage to manage your life. There is no freedom down that road. Stop running, stop hiding, stop pretending. Look at what you are, be honest about what you can see and step into the glorious light of this life. On that path is love and acceptance and the power to choose.

Fear cannot destroy you, only you can do that.

Before Jesus there was nothing you could do, after Him there's nothing you can't.

Fear denies your potential. Disagree.

Love costs

but so does fear,

& one of them
never pays you back.

We settle for escapism or busyness when we're too afraid of our talents.

Don't make excuses for fear, they will only establish markers for you to return to, bringing reassurance for small wickedness.

We must experience our survival of our fears.

We can't mature under fear.

You know the things that scare you the most?
God is there. Your mind has become persuaded of
otherwise but your mind is wrong.

The moment you become convinced fear is a liar,
your options change and your enemies change.

Fear can only prey on what isn't

entrusted to the light.

Let us throw off the shackles of fear and defense
and embrace the free-fall of tomorrow where anything
is possible; where stars aren't exclusive to the night sky
and voices are heard the planet round.

Darkness will try to swallow your light.
It can't, but it will try. Let it choke on your life.
Rip a hole in the blackness of evil by offering up
something real, something beautiful, something
bright, something you.

It could happen. The very thing you hope for, you could have it. What if that's exactly how it plays out? What if it's better than you expected? What if hope wasn't a traitor? What if hope wasn't threatening? What if you found out hope actually protects you and fights for you? What if you discovered it's not hope who sets you up for failure or disappointment? What if you realized it was fear who turned you against hope, that you became the enemy of what was good? What if disappointment and failure could burn up in the fires of true, valid, deep, lasting hope? What if you remained bathed in the warm light hope brings to the soul? What if you didn't spend time running from or dodging difficulty because hope empowered you to plow right through it? What if I told you hope fights for you and protects you? Hope keeps complacency and laziness at bay. Hope repels selfishness and fear. Hope makes you powerful. You can have it. It could happen.

Choose love.

Kick fear in the teeth and give away
what you have;

Life rewards such people.

Fear is selfish. Only love can convince you
the risk is worth it.

Giving something of yours is scary because it's
vulnerable but holding back should be scarier because
it will never be yours if you don't use it. Take the
risk, jump into the darkness, what you have
is strong enough to lift you.

Feeling fear and obeying fear are not the same thing.
Feeling fear comes with being human, obeying fear
comes with being a coward.

Any insecurity we feel is an external influence trying to broker agreement with us. We are not intrinsically insecure, we have to be persuaded to believe that. The moment you feel inferior or insignificant, something is trying to get you to believe that. It's not natural and the moment you recognize what's happening, you can choose to stay conscious of reality.

Love can be scary but fear is expensive.

Fear keeps us in ignorance. Those who are the most enlightened, who have the most wisdom and understanding are the bravest among us. They touched the same fear but they chose past it and discovered what was on the other side.

Fear and love are blinding. One limits you, the other expands you to infinity.

COURAGE

The willingness to be wrong makes one responsible with the power to be right.

Your weakness and fragility is not a liability but a blessing. You are designed for love and care and there are powers in this world which tend to that aim. Embrace the ways your walls crack and your blood leaks, they point to how you need love. Don't cover them up, let love in! Don't hide, come into the light. You are too precious to be cooped up in fear or pride. Your heart is soft for a reason, give yourself to that nature.

The world will not accept anything less than the real and authentic from you. If you dish out anything less, the world withholds its treasure.

We develop the ability to handle anything
when we resist the need to handle anyone.

Double mindedness will never let you stand up to
wickedness. There is no such thing as
an indecisive champion.

When the world holds a mirror to your blind spot,
have a look. There is a reward for those who learn how
to serve with all of themselves.

Faith and courage are rewarded with
gleaming opportunity.

A place to happen, to belong, that's what men are
looking for. They will follow leadership where they
get to matter and contribute. Forget the rules, men
follow courage, men follow passion.

Truth stands on commitment. Pick a side.
If you're wrong, be wrong. You can never be
right if you can't choose.

Demanding, domineering bosses are only allowed to
be so by those who give their quiet consent.
Tyrants are only allowed to be, it's not just their fault.
Community is a two-way street.

A fearless heart unlocks the fearlessness in others.

All the running away that we do is running away from
ourselves, our needs, our wants, our hopes and dreams.
We don't run from the devil, he's not that scary.
We run from desire, it's so costly and inconvenient,
we're taught how to get on without it.
Be all that you are. Let the opposition and
judgment come, truth will be what's left standing.
If your desire is true, you have nothing to be afraid of.

Embarassment is unexplored honesty.

What you take responsibility for,
you have authority in.

You will experience pain in life, either pain from
growing and learning or pain from compromise and
disappointment. The beauty is we get to choose
and the way we choose determines what we get to keep.

All He wants is for you to be fully alive, and it
takes fearlessness to live like that.

It's a lot easier not to care.
Once you don't care, it's a lot easier to hold back,
to refrain, to avoid and neglect and ignore.
But who wants to live in a world you don't care about?
It's a lot easier to give up. Once you give up,
it's a lot easier to accept defeat, to lose,
to surrender and quit and fail. But who wants to win
a game you didn't play? It's a lot easier to doubt.
Once you doubt, it's a lot easier to be skeptical,
to be offended, to question and challenge and deny.
But who wants a god they don't believe?

Have the courage to ask for what you want.
The worst thing that can happen is you're told no.
But imagine the best case scenario. What if what you
wanted could come true? What if you were justified?
What if you're worth it? Isn't just the possibility worth
the risk? Don't you owe it to yourself, to your Maker
and the world? Nobody benefits from your fear, no
one is better from your shrinking back. Your future
is not forged through passivity or inaction. It is the
brave nobility of hope which knocks on the doors
that open. The boring story of your regret is no legacy
to pass on, the daring legend of how you reached for
greatness is one to inspire and bequeath. You won't
leave stuff for your descendants, you will leave them
a story. You will leave them a code, a creed, a culture.
Leave them with hope, with the possibility that you
can have what you want, that dreams come true.
Don't just try, acquire your dreams.

Live in such a way that if men were their bravest and most honest, they would agree with your choices.

Truth is not a sunset to observe but an ocean of depths to plunge. Don't just applaud truth, get in the ring with Him and let Him knock you out.

It's not the pain you feel but the fear and hopelessness you believe as a result that destroys you. Pain is not the enemy, despair is. Don't fight discomfort, fight giving up.

Freedom isn't pain free, it's experiencing pain without having to hide it, without having to be sorry or ashamed for feeling it.

Purity
makes
you
bold.

It takes courage to admit you don't have it together. It takes humility to confess you don't feel worthy, you don't feel good enough, you're afraid you don't have what it takes. Anyone can pretend to be well-rounded, it's not hard to fool the people who care about appearances. It takes true character to acknowledge the mess your life might be in and call it what it is. It's these people who are privileged to find the end of themselves and consequently a solution to their problem that has more power than just to fix it. These people enjoy the taste of real life, of being a real person, of obtaining real victory. The pretenders only enjoy fake victories and even their joy is fake. Don't be afraid of having to start over, be afraid of arriving in a world that is not worthy of you. You are not here to appear like anything, you are here to BE loved, allow Him to take you.

If life is not scaring you, you're not
reaching for awesome. We have a Comforter
for a reason, you're meant to reach.

The thing you're too scared to say is the thing
choking out your voice in every other conversation.

For anything to last, for anything to increase,
it must be established in the light. For anything
to remain, for anything to stand, it must be planted
in truth and hope. We don't fight off the darkness,
we permit the light.

Giving something of yours is scary because
it's vulnerable, but holding back should be scarier
because it will never be yours if you don't use it.
Take the risk, jump into the darkness, what you
have is strong enough to lift you.

You know the things that scare you the most?
God is there. Your mind has become persuaded of
otherwise but your mind is wrong.

There's so much light, this world is bathed in luminosity.
It just takes courage to let go of the darkness we've
grown comfortable with to adjust to the vibrancy
and buzz of life in the light.

If you respect truth and refuse to
compromise her on your lips, she will give you the
power to stand before anyone and change the course
of matters. It's the truth tellers that
empower the heroes.

The solution for disconnection is not avoidance,
dead things buried decompose. Pull disconnection
into the light. Look at it. Be brave and work it out.

Anyone can be mean.
It takes courage to be kind.
Be brave,

show your heart.

If you want to be the person you're supposed
to be, let your fears crucify you. That kind of courage
will raise you from the dead.

You silence the voice of the accuser by casting your
lot with courage and resolve.

Sometimes love stabs. Are you willing to say the
piercing thing so truth can reach the tender spot?

Jump off the bridge before anyone else, there's
a special reward for the one who leaps into uncharted
territory. Risk is the lifestyle of the influential and
God holds His breath in the face of a hopeful wager.

When the fear of others doesn't scare us, we can
stick around and be brave.

Adventure is in the wild, she hides in the
unknown and challenges complacency. She rewards
those brave enough to risk it.

We aren't just dream chasers, dreams come true. We run after them because they can be caught, they must be caught. When you realize your dreams, blaze away. The world needs to see what it's like to get what you fight for; what you wait for, what you hope for, what you work for, what you train for. But more importantly, our young ones need to not just see people's dreams come true, they need to experience people in the world who believe in the power of their dreams because they came true. You can win the girl, dragons can be killed, dreams come true. When your day comes and it's here, meet it with all that you are and have your moment. What happens to you because of that instance will change people's lives. We owe the world the conviction of that moment. Get it.

Truth is costly and so is dynamite. But we need new roads, blow it up!

Have you been criticized lately for reaching for something beyond your depth? No? Reach Further.

Shave off the surplus of directions remove the excess doors; let another manage the options. You can only stand in the hallway or on the fence for so long. You were not designed to maintain several avenues of possibility. This is not an odds game, your future is not left to chance. Your destiny waits for you to commit. Your answers lie along the path of focused, un-compromised faithfulness.

Being falsely nice is just picking the colors of your prison walls. You were not designed to be nice but honest, not polite but kind, not well-behaved but authentically good.

THE SPIRIT WORLD

If equality is gained through shame, accusation and aggression, we only trade one form of bondage for another. The victim cannot vanquish the oppressor with the same violence she suffered, lest she turn into an oppressor herself. We cannot establish equality through aggression, we cannot fight our way into peace. Inequality was established and enforced via aggression and accusation, a contortion of the mind and a reduction of value. If we're to truly eradicate inequality, prejudice, racism and judgment, we must first find love within ourselves. When we have the compassion and grace to embrace ourselves, ugliness and all, we will have the power to love not just our neighbors but our oppressors. We can't just show them a better way, we must kill condemnation where it reigns the heaviest, in our own hearts.

If we want to let God out of the box,
we must let our neighbor out.

You are free to explore, free to express,
free to feel. The prison of conflict and struggle
is within. That you can't break out, that you can't
rise above, this is the prison and it is false. The
conflict has been resolved, He has made peace.
Everything belongs to you, do as you wish.

Passion and peace are not at war with each other.
Passion is the fire that burns, peace is the warmth
that emanates from the flame. All true passion
leads to peace; to the right order of things.

Don't get lazy discerning the spiritual and call your first impulse the Holy Spirit.

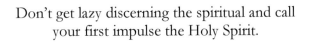
Boredom is rooted in selfishness.

When you liberate your conscience from having to respect other people's demons, you're ready to move in compassion to help.

The judgments you attach to people are what you end up having to fight against, not them.

When you learn the language of the spirit, you don't have to rely on people's words anymore. You wake up to the reality that what people say is a fraction of what they mean and sometimes it's altogether misleading. Words are not powerful unto themselves, without spirit they are dead.

It's easy and light. The moment your experience is other than this, you've taken up a spirit that was not intended for you.

Expression
must **never**
be perverted
by insincerity.

When we believe the lie that our blessings are because
of our merit, we can't look at them and enjoy them
in the light. We have to pretend like they're not there
lest our pride be exposed. Those who haven't bought
that lie get to openly enjoy the gift of their blessing.

What we try to hide will end up being hidden
from us, that's the nature of deception. What we secretly
agree with will secretly limit our world.

When your soul finds its deepest expression in your
union with God, you cannot praise highly anything
else you experience in this world. You can tell
those who haven't met intimacy with God by the
level of worship and praise they offer to men.

Failure is good for the soul, it removes the delusion
that we get to boast.

When you feel deep gratitude, be sure to express it;
a thank you card, a kind word, a prayer. It's important
that we honor gratefulness within us because it allows
us to experience more gratitude. When we stop
expressing the humility of appreciation and
thankfulness, we stop our hearts from
recognizing gratitude altogether.

We can't secure anything with a spirit of violence,
especially things like trust and respect.

If you don't know where to store your blessing,
look to your neighbor. In their need is its proper keep.

We desensitize ourselves with the myth of
separation. As long as we believe in the things that sever
us from other people, we can hide behind them and
remove ourselves from love's beckoning.

What is an atmosphere? It's that feeling created by
the past and current choices of the dominant spirit
that determines what's possible in a moment.

The anticipation of what is right around the corner
changes what is right around the corner.

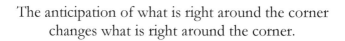

In a kingdom ruled by a King whose mere presence
enacts freedom, the son who takes ownership is the one
awarded power to uphold or change things.

Celebration moments are moving windows,
jump through when you can! You will be moved to the
degree that you move with the moment.

The need to blame comes from the lie that error must be punished.

The more I live honestly and the more I get to know people, the more I realize how normal I am. There's nothing wrong with me. The only thing that was wrong with me was I was convinced there was something wrong with me. There are no broken people, just broken beliefs.

What good is the gospel if it can only heal the sick and raise the dead but it cannot bring your heart into the light?

We can't stop God from enjoying us.
He sees us, He knows us, He enjoys us.
He's having a great time.

Be mindful of the way in which you associate
affection in your heart. The means by which you express
it is the means by which you will receive it.

The number of voices you can accommodate
in your life is: one. Listen carefully.

Freedom is
being bound to what you love.

You are a spirit. Don't just tell people what they need, give it to them. If you want someone to have peace, give it to them. If you want them to have courage, give it to them. Don't talk of good things, expose your relationship with goodness.

He will never stop coming through. As long as there is a "yes" in your breath for what you want, the power to manifest it will always come to your aid. There is no excuse for lack, ever. Wake up the giant within, he is hungry.

Do you want to experience the presence of God? Live and choose as if He is with you, you will awaken.

If I've learned anything from confronting
Wickedness in the world around me,
it's that identifying and condemning evil isn't enough,
we must bring the light. Hating builds nothing,
criticizing restores nothing, condemning heals nothing.
If you're on the side of light, you have to have more
than knowledge of the dysfunction. Find truth.
Find love. Find grace. Find forgiveness. Find the
power to reconcile the broken to the healer. It is in
demonstrating life that we destroy the works of
darkness, not calling darkness what it is. There's a
place for identifying what kind of evil is operating
but that is not enough, we must love
the hell out of this place.

Wisdom reveals herself to the lowly of heart,
you cannot know her and be proud.

I wonder how many people have made the agreement
that they aren't good at something because a critical
spirit convinced them it was so. Self-judgment is
a fruit of wickedness and to agree that you're not a
good dancer or singer or speaker or painter or mother
or son or spouse or worker in that critical spirit
actually establishes deception. You being "good"
at something, you performing to a standard, is not
flowing from the heart of God but evil. Literally,
declaring you're not good at something is wickedness.

The world is suspended in the posture of a question.
It is asking for the truth; not information
or knowledge but splendor.

We walk by faith not by sight. Enjoy
your time of sowing. What a blessing that
God has given you.

We are never void of spiritual
influence. There is no in-between place where
we are unoccupied. We were created to be filled
with something, to house God Himself.

What we all see and judge and pull from,
what we experience and deal with is not what is visible,
but what is invisible. It's the spirit, the root.

the gospel is a secret

only Jesus can tell you.

There is a guiding hand, sometimes you
win because you were destined to; the difference is
recognizing fingerprints.

You cannot combat evil spirits with
punishment; with detachment or aggression. A spirit
is undone by its opposite.

Don't shrink back from doing good or
opposing evil, this is food for your soul. Doing
what's right separates your consciousness from
what's wrong; it clears the path.

Passion and peace are not at war with each other. Passion is the fire that burns, peace is the warmth that emanates from the flame. All true passion leads to peace; to the right order of things.

Removing the expectation on quiet time with the Lord alleviates pressure and removes the sting of comparison. Keep going back to Him day in and day out, give Him faithfulness. Let the pressure of any certain outcome be on His shoulders.

It's not what you do but the spirit in which you do it that determines how people remember you.

Jesus doesn't help, he transforms. Jesus doesn't improve, He reanimates. Are you looking for bold and daring, cutting edge and sexy? Look no further, what you are looking for is Jesus. He is the boldest, sexiest, most daring man alive.

Revelation doesn't just tell you specific truth and uncover mysteries he shows you the pathways of knowledge to where you don't even need to know what you know, just where the door is.
Knowledge isn't information, it's access.

Be grounded, be truthful, do not speak if you have not cast your lot for the words you release. Influence is in the voice, wield this power faithfully and your environment will serve your steps. Plant the seeds of hope, life and wonder. Don't just close dark doors with your words, open bright ones, especially those which hearts pass through.

TRUST

If you have no one's trust, you have no influence.
You were made to change the world. Start with trust.

Intimacy isn't exactly divulging information, intimacy
is willingly being exposed to someone because of trust.

Hearts are surprisingly moldable. You're not
stuck, you just need to trust in something stronger
than fear to guide you.

Fear always comes to challenge trust; not that the thing itself is scary but that your Father won't come through.

Don't ask God to change your emotions, that is your responsibility. Your emotions are byproducts of your choices and beliefs. If you don't like your feelings, change where your trust is.

Having the guts to love oneself is true humility, this is trusting the Lord. Humility is not the debasement of oneself but the honor of another as you lay down your most precious gift: yourself.

Trust is not resignation,

it is
delightful,

absolute

exposure.

As long as you try to spare God from your ugly, it will remain ugly and messy and yours.

When you are persuaded of God's faithfulness in you, even your problems are glorious. Problems become opportunities for new and deeper ways to trust and delight in the Lord. The contrast becomes encouragement to lean more greatly on Him.

God is not afraid of your questions. But if your trust lies in an answer rather than a person, you will be estranged from love. This isn't about knowledge, it's about affection.

Don't expect to ever be rejected. May the experience catch you by surprise every time. Don't let your heart get used to negative occurrences, they must be strange and infrequent. As your heart learns to believe you're accepted and celebrated in every season, in every room, with every person, the world will start to accommodate your expectation.

The risk of trust is more productive than the security of skepticism.

Trust is not obligatory submission but a confident reliance. Trust is rest. Don't back down from the challenge life has brought your way. There are lessons to be learned. The challenge isn't whether you're strong but whether you trust. Every true lesson boils down to trust rightly placed. The power you need to reign in your liberation is found in your capacity to rely.

The most powerful son of the King is he whose trust is tested and nothing changes.

The differences we experience in each other are actually invitations for us to embrace trust, to embrace love rather than control.

The need to know what other people think of you is a direct indication of a way you don't trust God.

Do you trust God enough to love
who He made you to be?

Limits chosen by love protect the beauty
and depth of our experience. It's not always
ours to have it all. Sometimes refrain can keep
what's ours, ours. We were created with limits,
not to demean or control us but because this isn't
about absolute power; who has it and who doesn't.
This is about trust, who can and who won't.

Trust isn't unawareness, it's the power to keep
your heart open regardless.

You can't believe in something you don't want.

I find that sometimes the things
that scare us the most aren't our threats
or enemies but our dreams coming true.
Sometimes we're most afraid of getting what
we want because we're afraid of losing it.
The only way to cure that is to ENJOY the
blessing. Be grateful for your dream becoming
real, feel the pleasure that comes from it.
It's a vulnerable thing to let yourself experience
the delight of your desire manifesting.
The orphan fears it will be taken away, the son
does not. You are not an orphan be brave,
admit you want it and let others
celebrate with you.

Distrust is evidence that you're still trying to animate your old nature; to resurrect the person Jesus killed.

The one who bestowed us with desire and life also gave us the equipment we needed to manifest what we found within ourselves. Let us exhibit our trust in His faithfulness and justice by not relying on formula but on the spirit inside of us to create what is needed for the moment; it will be there.

You extend the grace you believe you have received.

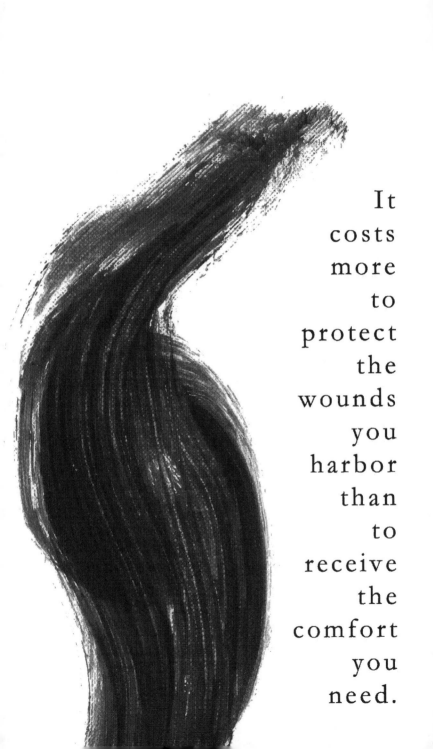

It
costs
more
to
protect
the
wounds
you
harbor
than
to
receive
the
comfort
you
need.

What if your guilt is unfounded? What if
your fear isn't true? What if your shame is a lie?
Love is real and He has already caught you.
Just give Him permission and He will
invalidate your need for walls.

You can't mess up God's plan for your life.
Do you know what God does with mistakes?
Do you know what He does with
ALL THINGS? He makes them work together
for your good. Take the risk.

Trust precedes influence. Build the fireplace
before you light the fire.

Every test is an opportunity, every temptation
a privilege. We are actually called to clarify our
allegiance and trust every time we are faced
with the choice between good or evil,
between trust and control.

Faith is vulnerable, hope shares itself.

ABOUT THE AUTHOR

Mike Maeshiro was born on Guam and raised in the small town of Hillsboro, Oregon. He is a graduate of YWAM, Japan and Bethel School of Supernatural Ministry.

Mike is an Advanced Ministry Training Instructor at Bethel School of Supernatural Ministry, a Spiritual Life Coach, an ordained minister, a prolific writer and an entrepreneur. He has built a solid and loyal social media following by posting daily thoughts and quotes of wisdom and inspiration. He explores emotional and spiritual health by posting thought-provoking content for his readers to wrestle with.

Mike's life mission is to raise the spiritual intelligence of the planet. It is a travesty to watch God's children suffer lack and oppression because they simply don't understand the world they live in. Mike seeks to remedy this issue and believes the day is coming where all spheres of society will operate differently because of the knowledge of the truth. From government policy to medical practice, Mike dreams of the day when the people intimately know the Spirit of Truth. **They will be free because they love Him.**

For further resources visit: www.mikemaeshiro.com

And follow Mike on:

 Mikemaeshiro

 Mike Maeshiro

 mikemaeshiro

 Mike Maeshiro

Made in the USA
San Bernardino, CA
20 May 2017